capulet mag

Capulet Mag

Volume 4
June 2019

Editors

Isabelle Rodriguez
Samantha Tetrault

Cover Art

"Let Your Love Grow"
Ink on Paper
Sophie Hamidovic

Print Design

Samantha Tetrault

Social Coordinator

Isabelle Rodriguez

CapuletMag.com
ISBN 978-0-359-73940-0

calling all capulets

Check yes Juliet,

This was supposed to be published in the Spring. It's July, so we'd just like to give a shout out to our biggest source of procrastination: Unrecommended. Unrecommended is a podcast about bad books. Bascially, it's the literary contribution nobody asked for, so you're welcome. Join us every Monday to lovingly trash talke *Twilight, 50 Shades*, and so much more.

Shameless promotion over.

As always, thank you for your continued support. Our lives have changed a lot since we first started this magazine. Isabelle graduated from college and got a big-girl job. Sam's moved (again). And she has new plans to move (again). She's also started her own business and it's actually kind of really amazing? Oh, and we're going to Paris (for real this time, fingers crossed).

All of this is a longwinded way of telling you that we're so grateful for your being there with us. And finally, to our writers and artists, thank you for trusting us with your creativity and passion. You're kinda amazing.

Check yes Juliet,

Isabelle & Sam

contents

She had to trust him out of her sight sometime.

Intersection

Fiction *Margery Bayne*

The first night Louise's grandson was back home, he was quiet and she was fretful. "Eat more than that" and "it's humid in here; I should pick up another fan at Wal-Mart" and "have you remembered to take your..." She struggled over the word 'anti-depressants' and settled on 'medication.'

"I'm fine," Teddy told her thrice over and some. When he announced he was ready to turn in half an hour after a dinner of pork chops – over cooked as Louise kept staring at him through the doorway as he napped on the couch – she swallowed back her comment about him barely being awake for more than an hour. The doctor said not to be surprised if he was sleepy.

He got halfway away up the steps before she blurted, "Leave the door open."

Teddy's grip twisted on the banister. Louise's eyes were drawn to the gauze wrapped around his wrists, hiding the marks.

"Yes, Gran," he said, in a solid whisper.

She tottered around the kitchen, wiping the table twice, rearranging the glasses in the cabinet for maximum space potential, and checking again nothing sharp had been left in the utensil drawers. This took all of eleven minutes. She had to trust him out of her sight sometime.

At thirteen minutes, she crept up the steps and peered slantways through his open doorway. Teddy laid on his side on his bed, head away from her so she couldn't tell if he were truly sleeping, but the movement of his torso meant he was drawing breath. She drew one too.

Fretfulness again reached it heights a week later when Louise was pressed into returning to work. "They need me, but...I could call out. I should call out. It's too soon," she said, taking and returning her purse to the coat hook.

Teddy, ever placating with 'fine' and 'okay' and 'whatever you want, Gran' snapped, "I promise not to off myself when you're gone, alright?" Shifting eyes away, he added, "I mean, it's just four hours, right? I can manage that."

"Five, plus travel," she countered, not telling him off for his tone. The spark of annoyed-anger was the most alive she'd seen him since... "You're sure you'll be okay? You'll call me if you start feeling...bad?"

He nodded and replied, a bit rueful, "I think I can make it." She pulled him into an embrace, cinch-like, nothing like the feather touches she had been treating him with.

Outside, at the house across the street, the blonde girl sat on the stoop reading. A blonde family had moved in while Teddy was hospitalized. Whenever Louise caught sight of either of them, something in her mouth turned sour, like a trained response. They and their yellow hair were like a signpost of before and after. This time, like every time, Louise swallowed it down and kept moving.

Brooke had adopted the hobby of people-watching since the move. Summer was a hard time to make friends when school was out and, frankly, she didn't want to. She hated the yard (too small), the street (too loud), and the house (missing someone). Only the sky was the same as what she knew and only during the day. There was too much city light at night to make out anything but the few brightest stars.

The house across the street was a mirror opposite replica to this thing her mom bought, except it was eggshell blue instead of moldy green. Brooke thought only an old woman lived there until a boy around her own age had shown up about a week ago and hadn't left since.

Her mom shouted for her from inside. After taking her time stretching, Brooke went in to find the woman standing in her bedroom doorway.

"What's this?" Her mom was looking at the stacked boxes with the unzipped suitcase plopped on top. "You said you were unpacked."

"I said I was as unpacked as I was going to be." Brooke crossed her arms.

Her mom sighed, ran a hand over her hair. "I'm worried about you," she said. It was worse than being yelled at.
Brooke cocked her head, didn't look at her, and said, "Then maybe you shouldn't have taken me away from him." She entered her room and shut the door.

Louise jabbed the door with her hip to get it open since the wood was swollen with the air's humidity. The wall ornament crucifix fell to the desktop with an echo-y clatter. Louise picked it up and tapped it with her fingernail. It was colored to look like stained wood, but all this time it was plastic. She replaced it on the nail hanging from the plaster.

She sat in her chair, tugging her replacement's post-its from the edge of the monitor, inspecting them in turn, and trashing them. She opened a spreadsheet on the old computer and started next month's schedule for the fellowship hall. She got fifteen minutes into her work – fifteen minutes of setting things straight and mild mental hurdling that set her blissfully away from her worrying – when Pastor Dan knocked at the door.

Pastor Dan was young, new to the church, and insisted on using his first name with his parishioners.

"Hello, Louise," he said, pausing before her name as if taking a second to recall it. He insisted on using everyone else's first names too. "Glad to have you back."

"Glad to be back," she said, keeping her fingers typing.
It wasn't her place to bar him from the church office, but he stepped further in uninvited. "How's your, um, grandson doing?"

"He's home now."

"Forgive me, I've heard conflicting information on why he was hospitalized."

"You mean gossip," Louise said.

"Gossip tends to be many congregations' biggest faults." He tucked his hands in his pockets and shrugged. A spiteful flare for the casual young man shot through her nervous system.

"He had an accident," she said.

Not deterred by the obvious bluntness, he said, "I'm still trying to learn the congregation. He lives with just you?"

"His father's work keeps him away. And his mother passed away when he was young."

"Oh. I'm sorry. How did she –?"

"Accident." That was all Louise would say about her late daughter-in-law. Sarah was a sweet enough girl, yet awfully moody. Teddy was too much like her.

"We'll keep your family in our prayers," Pastor Dan said, finally stepping out.

It may have been guilt that clung to Brooke like sweat that kept her hiding well past midnight, but hunger eventually drove her to creep downstairs. She never expected her mom to still be awake on the couch, sounding sniffle-y.

"Oh, oh," Mom squeaked when she heard Brooke on the creaky bottom step. Brooke leaned up on her tiptoes to see what Mom was holding. She only caught a glimpse, but that's all she needed. She knew what it was: the family photo. The one in the big frame that used to be in the center place on the fireplace mantel at the old house: Brooke at six years old and gap-toothed; Mom and Dad flanking her; all three with stupid smiles and worse haircuts.

Brooke hadn't seen her mother cry since the funeral. She had been so stony-edged, commanding Brooke through the move. Now, her mom rubbed her eyes to remove any evidence of tears. Brooke kind of hated herself. She hated that she couldn't will her feet to move the few feet to give her Mom a hug. There were a lot of things that should be said. Instead, "I was just getting a glass of water."

Back upstairs, Brooke left the glass to sweat on her dresser, laid down to sleep, and promised herself to do better tomorrow.

Louise hated the psychiatrist visits because Teddy came out red-eyed and with a renewed dedication to silence. What could Teddy feel safe telling a stranger that he couldn't tell her?

Today, he was quiet and avoided eye contact.

"Did you tell Dad?" he asked on the way home, just as they took the turn by the graveyard. "He's not coming is he?" Louise twisted her grip on the steering wheel. "I'm here," she said. She'd always been; she'd been the only one to never leave.

"I know. I ... I know." He reached over and plucked at her sleeve like he'd done when he was little and trying to get her attention. "I know."

At home, she set herself into the work of tidying up, idle hands and all that. And she was always less worried when she had something to do. She sent Teddy out to collect the mail under the same idea.

Louise had a set routine to keep her home organized and clean, having lived there since she got married. The demographics of the home shifted through to the years: just her and her husband, then baby made three. Of course, the baby grew up and moved out and the husband had a heart attack. Alone wasn't exactly how she imagined growing old, but now she had Teddy.

Danny hadn't turned out to be much of a father. Louise

couldn't account for Sarah's upbringing. Louise would get this one right. She wouldn't lose Teddy too.

She'd tell Teddy she didn't blame him and that she'd listen to anything he'd want to say and try harder to understand... as soon as he got back from getting the mail.

She checked through the front window's lace curtains. Teddy was at the end of the walk, by the mailbox, envelopes clutched in hand, as the blonde girl from across the street talked at him. When he got back in, Louise asked lightly, "What took so long?"

"We have new neighbors across the street," Teddy said with the astonishment of having learned something new. "And Brooke – I mean – there's a girl my age there. She was just introducing herself."

Teddy was blushing. Louise took the mail from his hands. She'd tell him all those things when the moment was right.

Flipside

Poetry *Jocelyn Royalty*

5 PM. Jumping jacks. You are in your bedroom
and it's still early   but daylight-chagned into your
favorite black nail polish
the one you buy at the Taft   after work
when you're feeling sexy
or like you're daylight changing
and you want something to staple you down

You go on adventures to the grocery store. Gas station,
fuselage. You go to the community garden and
make soup in the greenhouse kitchen.
        The homeless man that sleeps on the dahlia beds
        says *hey*, says he thinks your spinal cord is pretty,
says his parents came to the US
        on a potato boat. You say,
mine got here by tying ten thousand homing pigeons to their RV.

        Who's got a compass now?
Who's *loca* now?

        5PM. This city, strung out like losing hair.
        You paint your nails.

        You go to a 24-hour chapel in a big t-shirt with holes
        and profess your love for a bottle of nail polish. Me
too. Your shoes are blue

and they come to a point.
        You're American!   baby. Made of pure sangre
        and ER visits. You come to a point.
You've got nothing but dahlias and daylight savings
        Stored in the loose floorboard.
                        Me too.

Koi

Poetry *McKenzie Teter*

Swimming stupidly in circles
The koi do not seem to mind

There is water
There is food
That is enough

This pond will never grow any bigger
There will never be anything new to discover

But yet
The koi do not seem to mind
The sameness they live in
Or the sameness they are fed
Today as the day before
And before
And before

There will never be anything new to discover
This pond will never grow any bigger

That is enough
There is food
There is water

The koi do not seem to mind
Swimming stupidly in circles

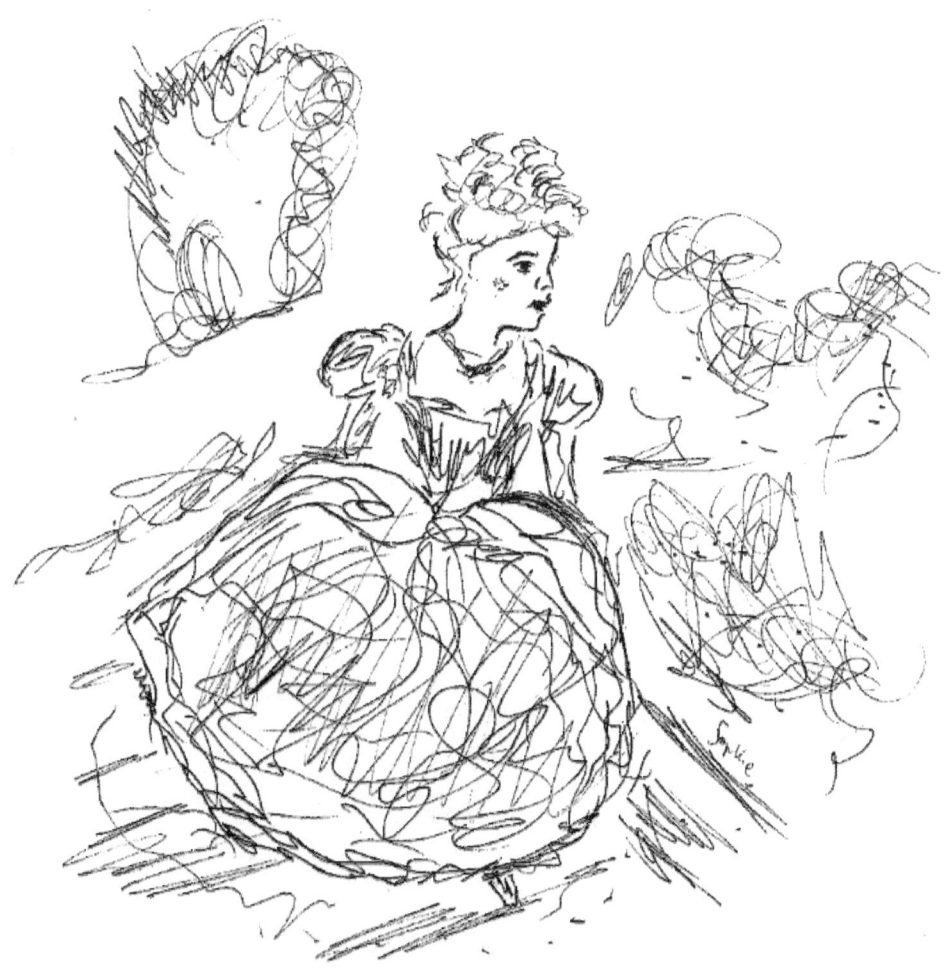

Cinderella en Noir
Ink on Paper *Sofia Rybkina*

Five Things About Parkinson's Disease
Poetry *Greta Starling*

i.
they don't know if it can be passed down,
from my grandmother to my mother to me,
or this curse, like lightning, only strikes once.
if my life is a coin toss
or a punnett square.

ii.
they don't know the magic formula.
all the work we put in just to be healthy,
eat this but not that, exercise this much,
meditate daily and take these vitamins,
might not change anything in the end.

iii.
even if i knew if i had it,
waiting for me to grow and weaken,
i wouldn't be able to stop it.
just wait until it took me over,
wait to lose myself piece by piece.

iv.
they don't know if an answer is even out there
if it's worth it to keep looking
even if i give my money, if i give my time,
they don't know if they could do anything with it
if anything in the world could do anything to the disease.

v.
i know the things that i miss
and the things i hope i never have to.
my grandmother's laugh, my mother's silly made-up songs,
my handwriting,
they have to search because i know what happens if they stop.

The panic settles like a dark mist snaking around my throat and squeezing my soul from my body.

The Attack

Fiction *Kristina Fedeczko*

My heart races and my stomach clenches as the air inside the plane freezes. A cold, paralyzing sensation washes over my body as I think of the coming battle. The panic wants to murder me. I'm going to die.

"You look nervous."

I don't look over at the voice. The panic coursing through my veins immobilizes my body. The panic settles like a dark mist snaking around my throat and squeezing my soul from my body.

This is not the first time I've had a panic attack in public. The first time I was at the movie theater and the actress on screen was trapped in a sinking boat. Watching her struggle against the rushing water made my throat close like I was drowning along with her. The second time was when I was taking the LSAT. I realized during the reasoning section of the test, that my score didn't matter. I would die at some point and not even the LSAT mattered. The third time was during my grandmother's funeral. I couldn't shake the image of her dying alone in the hospital room. After that, I lost count of the number of times panic held my heart hostage.

"Are you going to pass out or something?"

I hear the voice but I don't know who it belongs to. I'm traveling alone, but that's not what bothers me. What makes my heart beat faster (and not in a good way) is flying. I'm positive that the plane is going to fall out of the sky and I'll die.

I press my lips together and hold in the scream. I scream when I get a panic attack, but I try to keep the panic under control in public. Only in the safety of my apartment do I throw my head back and scream. My neighbors probably think I'm crazy or maybe they think I'm like all the other stressed out law student scattered around Cambridge.

"Hey, are you okay?"

No, I'm not okay. I will never be okay. I am dying. Doesn't anyone see that? My soul is leaving my body. The panic is winning yet again.

Just like that, the panic subsides like an ocean wave. Now, exhaustion clings to my limbs. My shoulders slump and I loosen my jaw. I run my hands along the side of my face trying to release the lingering panic from my mind.

"You're looking better," says the voice.

I finally look towards the voice to see a woman. She looks to be a few years older than me with curly hair, brown eyes, and a kind smile.

"Yeah," I say. I shift in my seat. I need to get a handle on my panic. It's getting embarrassing how many times people look at me like I'm crazy, ask if I am okay, or if they need to call 911.

The woman leans closer to me and whispers, "Don't worry. I get panic attacks too."

I blink at her. I don't know what to say. My gut reaction is to hug her and announce to the entire plane there are more of us out in the world, but that might be a little weird.

"I get panic attacks when I think about dying," I say.

"I get panic attacks when something triggers my PTSD," the woman says.

The plane moves forward. The plane about to take off. Isn't taking off the most dangerous part of a flight? Or is it the safest? I can't remember and the panic dances around my heart once more.

The plane starts to pick up speed. We race towards the end of the tarmac. The plane lifts off the ground and into the clouds. The woman opens up a magazine she brought with her and I stare outside the small window at the clouds. I don't ask about her PTSD and she doesn't ask me about dying.

My gut reaction is to hug her and announce to the entire plane there are more of us out in the world

The Two Kinds of Women in the World

They both died domestic deaths,
The homewrecker and the housewife.
Both with their heads on the cool
Grate of an oven.
A fuck you to t fifties.

That era of aprons like straitjackets,
that gleamed white.
Like carnivorous teeth, that swallowed up
The lives of women.
Ate them as they cooked.
The mistress worked as an ad-writer, came up
With the slogan "Mr. Kipling's
Exceedingly good cakes,"
Would they have killed themselves
If they didn't know how to turn
On an oven in the first place?

There are two kinds of mothers in the world,
The Sylvias who switch on the gas
But fold a thin blanket under
The kitchen door sill.
So that it won't poison their children in the next room.
And the Assias,
Who take their children along with them.
Like stray punctuations on their epitaphs.

On Ted Hughes, Sylvia Plath, and Assia Wevill
Poetry *Anushka Joshi*

In their own ways, protected
Their children.
The first from death,
The second from life.

The man whom
Leaves a woman
With the tumorous instinct for death
Growing in her gut,
Faster than a fetus.

Gave up hunting but never
Quite lost the habit of slaughter.

Even if
He considered suicide, he would
Abandon the thought,
Abandon the house,
Abandon the children there.

Go instead for a walk
Or to make a call,
Forgetting to switch off
The gas at all.

What Washes up in Floods
Nonfiction   *Katie Licavoli*

I spent the first eight years of my life on a dead-end road tucked away in the outskirts of the DFW Metroplex. There were many interesting things that happened on that road, but one of the oddest memories I have is of something my friends and I found washed up in a nearby creek one summer afternoon.

The creek flowed under a wooden bridge that led to the entrance of my street. Most of the time this creek was nothing more than a dribbling stream of water, but when the spring rains came unpredictably pouring in and the formerly dried-up clay couldn't drink up the water fast enough, it could quickly turn into an overflowing river within a matter of days.

When the rains were in full force, I remember I'd watch from the school bus window in the morning to see how high the water was when we crossed over the bridge. Then, in the afternoons when the bus would haul me back over that bridge towards home, I'd once again look out the window to see how much higher the water had grown.

Once, during these rains, I remember my mom let my sister and I sleep in during a school day. Upon waking, I'd wandered from my room confused and groggily wondering where my mom was and why in the heck she hadn't woken me up for school. I found her holding a cup of coffee looking out our back window, I could see her eyes were directed towards our pond that appeared to have swollen overnight. She told me the creek had risen so much it'd completely flooded the entrance to our road. We were trapped. My mom might have been concerned, but all I heard was that I didn't have to go to school for a few days.

My mom then bundled my sister and me in our rubber

I'd once again look out the window to see how much higher the water had *grown.*

rain boots and vinyl raincoats and we all walked the three-quarters of a mile down our street to join our other imprisoned, onlooking neighbor's. We stood there alongside each other at the water's edge, speechless, looking out over the flooded fields and wondering where under all that water was our road and the old familiar bridge.

I remember there being two of these major floods during my short eight years of living in Texas. I also remember that these floods were an even bigger oddity because in my neighborhood we commonly had the opposite problem occurring: the whole place was bone dry.

We referred to this bone-dry experience as 'drought season.'

I remember how the days of drought season seemed to drag on and how there never seemed to be enough water to go around. All the adults on the street, my parents included, would go on and on about the *damn drought* that was happening again. They'd compare how many feet their wells had fallen, and, after a while, we'd all keep count of the number of days that had passed since the last drop of rain.

Before long, each household would have to preserve water and I'd watch as the little grass in everyone's yards would brown, and the ponds and creeks would dry up, leaving mounds of cracked, dehydrated clay to take over the landscape.

One summer, months after a flood had come and gone and when we were right amid another drought season, my neighborhood friends and I got the idea that it could be fun to go see what might have been left behind in the creek bed from the previous flood.

We reached the bridge and just as we'd suspected, there wasn't a drop of water under it. We climbed our way down into the gulley where the water would usually be and followed along the creek bed. We came across left behind trash, twisted branches, a few fallen trees, and other odds and ends that were no surprise. After a while of finding nothing exciting, I remember feeling as though our adventure might be adventure-less when suddenly we all saw something unfamiliar a few feet ahead. It looked like a large heap of dirt embossed white fur. It stopped me dead in my tracks and sent my mind wondering what in the heck the mysterious heap of fur was, and more importantly, was it dangerous?

I couldn't tell from where I was standing if it was alive or dead but I knew which I preferred. Dead meant I wasn't about to get attacked by this freaky looking thing. Coming across a dead animal wasn't all that weird for my friends and I. Whether we were walking around in the woods or even through some of our own yards, each one of us at one time or another had stumbled upon dead snakes, spiders, armadillos, skunks, and even a few newborn kittens that coyotes had gotten to.

This giant mass of white fur, however, was a new one for all of us. Our first fear was that it might be Cowboy, Brandon and Ethan's 10-year-old dog that was always wandering around the neighborhood. But the mass looked bigger than Cowboys size and the fur looked curlier. After weighing our options, we did a unanimous vote and elected Brandon, the oldest yet far from the bravest boy in our group, to check things out.

Toting along with a stick for protection, we watched as Brandon slowly and cautiously made his way towards the mass of fur. When he was a few feet away, he poked it. Then he poked it again, and again... I held my breath in anticipation, yet the fur mass didn't appear to move. A second later I heard the "HOLY SHIT" come from Brandon's mouth followed by, "YOU GUYS HAVE GOT TO SEE THIS!"

We all came running and when I reached Brandon's side, I realized he had a good reason to use a cuss word. In front of me, with its dried-up tongue flopping out to one side and its body in a twisted, distortedly uncomfortable looking position was a dead llama.

It looked as though it had been there awhile, black flies were buzzing in and out of the eyes and parts of it were decomposing. Its fur was a dirty white color, and even I could tell it had to be at least a young adult or maybe even full-grown llama by its size.

Brandon threw his stick at it and it bounced off and ricocheted to the side. He grabbed another stick and poked at it again. The smell was that of roadkill that's been sitting and baking in the sun for days. It was unbearable, yet we all stood there unable to peel our eyes away from the dead llama. I'm not sure why my friends kept staring but, for me, I found the creature fascinating. It was the first time I'd ever in my whole eight years seen a real-life llama, even if it was dead.

Brandon then poked at its side trying to see if he could lift it up. After a few moments, he lifted a part of the body a few inches off the ground and what I saw underneath surely should have sent my stomach hurling but my brain told me to take off running instead. Right before I high tailed it I watched, only momentarily, as part of the decaying llama broke off and flopped back on the ground while a sea of black and white bugs came flying in and out from it.

Before the first flying bug could touch my face, I was gone. I didn't stop running or look back behind me to see who was joining me until I was standing back on the bridge over the creek bed. I'd even half ran/half climbed my way up the side of the gulley to the bridge faster and more calculated than I ever knew I could do. As I stood there on the bridge catching my breath and wiping away the sweat beads that formed on my forehead, I saw my friends coming up one by one over the side of the gulley. They were just as out of breath as I was.

While I stood there trying to slow my breathing, the dead llama scene kept replaying over and over in my head. I decided right then I'd do my best to stay as far away from any future dead animals I saw. Nature could do its thing in peace from there on out.

**I didn't stop
running
or look back
behind me
to see who was
joining me
until I was standing
back on the bridge
overtop the
creek bed.**

the
sun
sets
but
it
also
rises

Death in the Afternoon

Poetry McKenzie Teter

Hemingway couldn't beat it

The words pumped in his veins
And gathered in his head
But wouldn't pour out his fingers

So he blew them all over the walls
At the age of 61

Gave his art his heart
But couldn't make it love him back

The sun sets
But it also rises

Death in the afternoon,
On a Sunday no less,
The worst kind.

A Passionate Love Letter to Twilight

Nonfiction *Samantha Tetrault*

I discovered Stephanie Meyer's *Twilight* at the ripe young age of 12 years old. My dad accidentally bought me the third book, *Eclipse*, as part of my middle school's mandatory reading initiative. I opened the book none-the-wiser, finding myself in Bella's kitchen. As expected, Charlie was in the living room watching the game. (Bella has to do all the housework in *Twilight* because the narrative subscribes to traditional male-female household roles.)

Bella and Edward were bickering about college. This would be a conversation they'd have again and again. It wasn't until later (circa $20,000+ in student loan debt) that I'd realize just how good Bella had it. She found a vampire boyfriend and he was willing to pay for an Ivy League education? Sign me up for a clingy boyfriend if it means a life free from student debt.

Because I didn't know who Bella was, let alone why she was so fixated on Edward's willingness to pay for Dartmouth (or was it the University of Alaska?), I shut *Eclipse* then and there. I didn't open it for another few months when I'd finally decided to read the series from the beginning.

Before we get into this long-winded rant about *Twilight* that nobody asked for, I need to discuss my love of reading. I was always a reader. Like most kids from divorced parents, I spent a lot of time alone in my room. I was a weird, quiet kid, and one of my favorite things was reading romance books. Especially romance books about princesses. I had already made my way through the "older kid" section at Barnes & Noble, so I was slowly stumbling into the world of young adult.

I have a bad habit of taking things a bit − ahem − too

far. Exhibit A: the *Divergent* tattoo on my ribcage. But I'll digress to a less permanent example that doesn't involve permanent body art. When I was in middle school, I was obsessed with this book series about girls in boarding school. This was at the peak of the *Zoey 101* Era (circa 2004 ad), so it had a lot going for it already. What I'm trying to say is this book wasn't just fiction to my impressionable mind. This was when I assumed Aaron Carter was my soul mate, if that gives you a clearer picture. This book series was The Coolest Thing I'd ever read, and I tucked this information away at the back of my mind for later.

The opportunity never really presented itself, naturally, since my family wasn't exactly of the northeastern elite. But not to be deterred, I forced the opportunity myself. That's right, I shipped myself off to boarding school. Sure, it might have been a bit more involved than this, but I can confidently say my determination to go to a preppy, snooty boarding school in the northeast stemmed from that very book series that shall not be named.

We're almost to the *Twilight* part, I promise.

This is just a long-winded way of saying I take books really seriously. So when eighth-grade me finally opened *Twilight* for the first time, oh boy, she was in for a wild ride. I devoured the book like it was the most amazing thing I'd ever gotten my hands on – because it was. It evoked a passion for the dark and twisty that I didn't even know I had. These thoughts I can't decode, amiright?

Finally, we've made it to the part where I start defending *Twilight*. Put your pitchforks down, people. Let me preface this by saying that I understand *Twilight* is not an example of a healthy, thriving relationship. I understand and rationalize this, and I've decided I like it anyway. I recently revisited the series as an adult, both physically and figuratively. I mean physically because I stopped at a grocery store in Forks, Washington to pee, and that's probably the closest I'll ever get to living in a young adult novel. I mean figuratively because I recently re-

read each chapter one at a time, letting myself absorb the gloriously simple language like the shining example of youth culture that it is. Since taking both of these journeys (the grocery store bathroom and the re-reading), I've come to the conclusion that the book is the most glorious symbol of not giving a damn. Bella lacks critical thinking skills, yet she's willing to throw herself off a cliff just to get what she wants. That's the kind of blind ambition I've adapted into my own life.

You could make the argument that Bella is written as an "everygirl," but she was also written as someone who knows what she wants and is willing to get it at literally any cost. Does she take it too far? Definitely. Nobody told her to ditch Alice and go to that ballet studio to get her leg broken and blood sucked, but my girl is a go-getter. She did it anyway because she's brave and she does what she has to do to get what she wants.

In a dark, twisty way, this blatant lack of self-concern for the seemingly "rational" choice resonates with me. I applied to boarding school despite my complete lack of connections, amazing grades, or (the big whammy) money. I got rejected from every school my first year of applying. How dare those big-name schools with acceptance rates lower than Yale not accept my public-school, scholarship self? But, like Bella, I didn't give a gosh darn crap. I was back at it the next year, applying with an even stronger application than before and not taking no for an answer. I applied to eight schools. I only got into one. One was enough.

Bella goes after what she wants, no matter the cost. So do I, even if it means taking a year off from my dream school to travel the world, turning down said dream school six months later, dragging myself out of another bout of depression, quitting my day job to work for myself, or even just taking a goddamn day off.

In *Breaking Dawn*, Bella jokes that self-control is her superpower. In a lot of ways, I think that this is my superpower too. Self-control to get through college with two jobs, self-control to start my own business when my day job just spirals me deeper into my depression, self-control to just not care what I'm "supposed" to do.

This is waxing a bit too poetic for a *Twilight* essay.

Even for me.

It goes without saying that *Twilight* gets hate just because it's something liked by teenage girls. As a teenage girl who liked Twilight and then pretended she didn't all through high school, I'm tired of it. While I don't necessarily want a romance that looks like a young adult love triangle, I have a lot to thank *Twilight* for.

At the very least, it reminded me that I wasn't alone with my dark and twisty feelings. As an adult, I can look back on that girl reading about Forks in her room alone at night. I can thank Bella for igniting a bright, hot spark underneath me, and for reminding me that the most wonderful things happen sometimes if you just go blindly into that twilight.

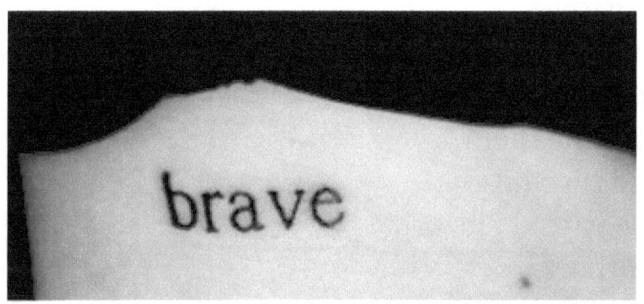

PS. I wish I was kiding about
the *Divergent* tattoo.

Ink on Graphite *Blossoming* *Sophie Hamidovic*

The Marriage
Poetry *Anushka Joshi*

Scott and Zelda once spent an hour
In the revolving door of a hotel-
Just another jazz age prank.
Like jumping into the fountain at Union Square.
Later the accusations,
The sanatoriums,
The burning to death,
And the death by drowning
In endless glasses.
For now the mouth of misery
Was still muzzled.
Can you imagine them
Turning and turning
Echoing the earth in its orbit.
Always returning
To where they had been seconds ago,
Two detectives investigating their own footprints
In rehearsal for regret.

Christian Slater Can't Do a British Accent

Nonfiction *Aurora Dimitre*

My first experience with the Robin Hood story was with the Disney animated version. My first experience with the Robin Hood story when I gave a shit was the BBC series, which ran from 2006-2009. To put it into perspective, I sobbed so hard when Allan-a-Dale died at the end of season three[1] that I had to ward off an errant phone call and call the person back later. I think I was twelve.

I don't know what my mother's first experience with the Robin Hood story was, but I do know that her favorite is *Prince of Thieves*. Post-BBC series, I was just hungry for more Robin Hood, even if Jonas Armstrong wasn't going to be Robin. Suddenly, Allan was lame[2], and I was throwing myself into every adaptation I could get my hands on. Naturally, *Prince of Thieves* was one of those—it came pretty highly recommended by my mother, who not only loves Alan Rickman but also Christian Slater.

It should be mentioned that I also really love Christian Slater.

I recently rewatched *Prince of Thieves*, and this is what compelled my spiral back into Robin Hood. In rewatching, I noticed a couple of things. First of all, it's long as hell. Seriously, this bitch is two and a half hours long. It's got some good action scenes and some funny bits, but if a movie outlasts my computer battery, it's probably too long[3]. There's also the matter of Kevin Costner and Christian Slater's accents or lack

1   Whoops, spoiler alert.
2   The BBC series pretty much made Allan the traditional Will Scarlett. Will was still a character, he was just different.
3   Or maybe my computer battery is just shit, but po-tay-to, po-tah-to.

This is what compelled my spiral back into Robin Hood

thereof. Sometimes. There's the very 90's soundtrack. Didn't you know? Every movie from the 90s had to spawn a hit song about a woman wailing about something.

As you can tell, I loved it.

And it made me think. I started asking, "You know, what draws us to stories like Robin Hood?" Seriously, what makes us tell this story over and over and over, with varying degrees of seriousness[4], with varying degrees of success?

If somehow you've gotten through life without hearing about Robin Hood, the basic premise is this: a nobleman returns from the Holy Land after fighting in the Crusades. Oh shit, he realizes his home country of England is a shithole now. He becomes an outlaw. Robin Hood starts up a merry band of outlaws, including Will Scarlett, Allan-a-Dale, and Little John[5]. It's a tale as old as time. Steal from the rich, give to the poor. There are various subplots and other things going on (the love affair with Maid Marian, Will betraying him at one point, and so on), but the main thing is just to steal from the rich and give to the poor.

Most of us are not what we would call wealthy. Even if you're comfortable right now, you probably wouldn't be doing so hot if suddenly your house burned down, or your health took a drastic turn for the worse[6], or you were unable to work. The fact of the matter is, even though we do live in the best time period in all of human history, and we are not nearly as fucked as medieval peasants were, the one percent is the one percent no matter the time period.

There are some people who are strictly law-focused. It doesn't matter if it's morally right. All that matters is if it's according to the law or against the law. But, I think most of us aren't law-focused. Most of us are justice-focused. If, say, Jeff Bezos's house burned to the ground, he would be fine. He owns

---

4   Hello, Men in Tights.

5   Little John is never little. That's the irony of his name. Though I would live a version where Little John is played by Peter Dinklage.

6   Especially if you're in America with its health insurance hellscape.

Amazon. If a Kardashian got cancer, they would be fine[7]. They have the kind of cash to pay for top-level treatment. All of this security is because they do something that people give them a lot of money for. This isn't just relevant with people I'm not a huge fan of. I'll do someone I really like. Say Kirk Hammett[8] shattered his hands and couldn't play the guitar anymore. This would be a tragedy, and I would be really sad, but if he couldn't play in *Metallica* anymore, he would not be out on the streets. He would probably be watching old monster movies or something. I dunno what he does in his free time.

Most of us aren't that lucky. I don't own a house, but my parents own theirs—and one of the main reasons why they're doing well financially is that they don't have to pay rent or mortgage payments. If that house that they got for twenty-four thousand dollars in 2001[9] burned to the ground, it would hurt them[10]. If I or one of my family members got cancer, the bills would suck ass. If my father, the primary breadwinner of the family, was unable to work, that's like eighty thousand dollars a year they're out. Could they keep going on my mom's regular teacher's salary[11]? Well, they live in rural North Dakota and have their house paid off, so probably, but they wouldn't be as comfortable. And if they lived somewhere with a higher cost of living with their three kids[12], things would look bleak.

So if, say, some weird vigilante rich person went and robbed Jeff Bezos and got away with it—would we really be all that upset about it? Say you opened up Twitter one morning and you saw that Danny DeVito had robbed the fuck out of Jeff Bezos, and then walked along the streets and gave out cash to everyone he passed. Wouldn't that just be the tightest shit? That would be so cool. We would all hardcore support Danny

---

7   Like, assuming they didn't die from cancer.
8   Lead guitarist for the band *Metallica*.
9   Thanks 2001 housing market and also rural North Dakota.
10   This is also kind of likely, considering my family is full of idiots and we have a wood burner.
11   Somewhere around 40k, I think.
12   Though I'm hopefully gonna be outta there soon.

DeVito in this situation. We would hide him if he came through our towns, the FBI on his tail. We would support him because we knew that he cared.

The thing about a folk hero like Robin Hood, who was born a nobleman who had all the privilege in the world, is that he gave all of that away. Beyond the fact that most adaptations have him rub the new sheriff the wrong way, he leaves his place of privilege for two reasons: justice and freedom. He lives among his men in Sherwood Forest because together they're free. They're pretty much a commune, to be honest, which does speak to the wish that communism would just work, man, but once you get bigger than the commune stage it ain't gonna work ever, and there will always be people who want more power. But anyway, there's a freedom in that outdoor living. It speaks to the romanticism of living in the forest, away from rules that don't make any sense and away from people who try and keep you under their boot.

More than that, Robin Hood is someone from inside the system pushing against it. Maybe Danny DeVito isn't the best example here because I don't think Danny DeVito's ever been a part of the system in the first place.

The reason I think Robin Hood has lasted so long is because people know that the system is broken. People have always known that the system is broken, and if someone who benefits from that system realizes this and leaves the system— well, then there's hope.

In Bloom
Ink on Paper *Sophie Hamidovic*

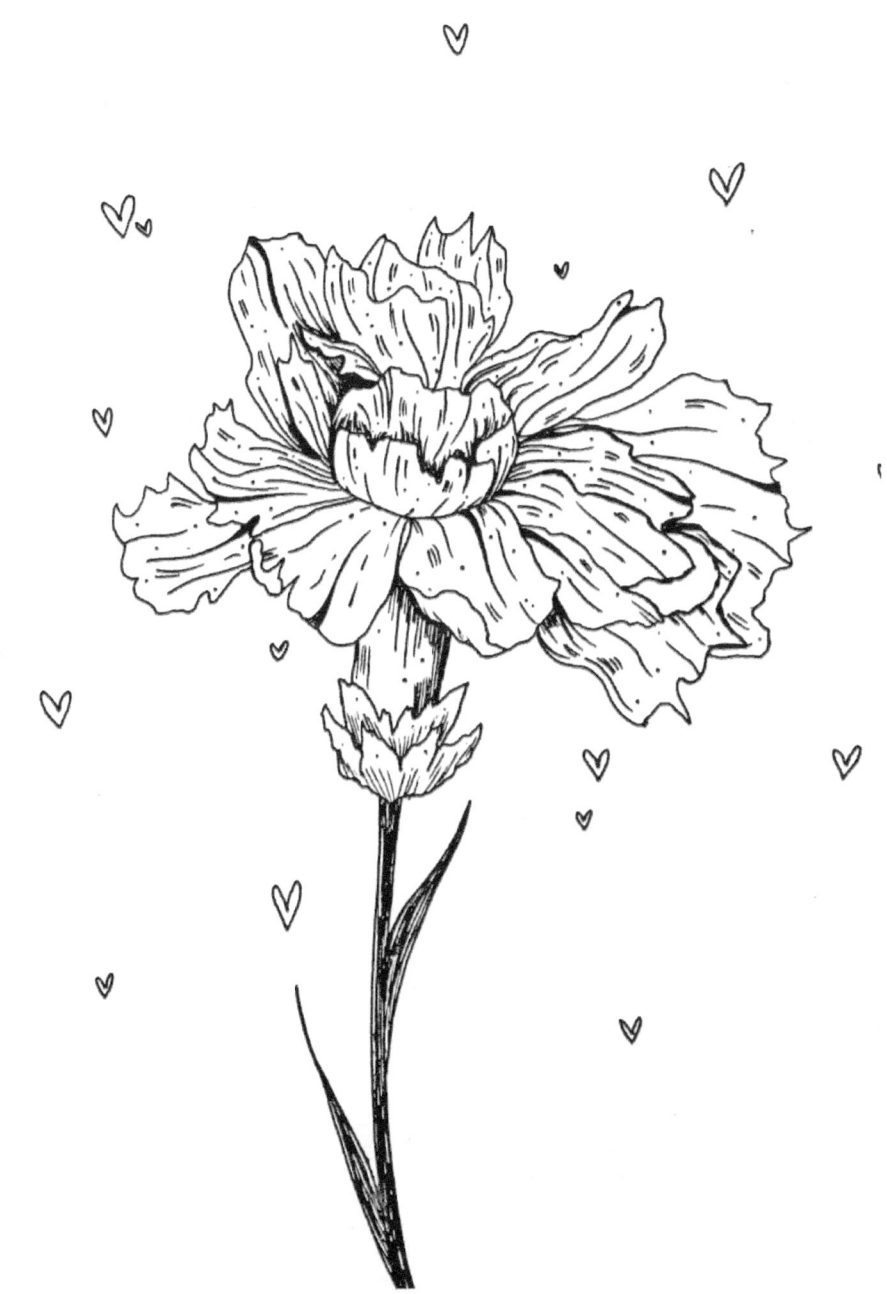

Portrait of Penelope at the Loom

Poetry *Arielle Hebert*

When I left, you became an island.
Shut up in our room all day,
you wrapped the woven cloth
around your naked body,
undressed under the moon,
unraveled the forest of threads.

You told yourself you were waiting for me,
but it was war you waited for, the end
of bodies that arrived in bags,
carried off ships by shoulders
you prayed would not bear me home.

For twenty years, your hands
filled, emptied of threads.
For the first few, all you imagined was war.
For the last, all you imagined were women,
trouble, seaweed hair and salty fingers.

Calypso and Circe meant nothing, nothing.

No wonder you turned to weaving
for comfort, to create
and destroy something in the same day.

Even after my return,
you kept the fires burning.
Torches multiplied your shadow
on the wall and you danced with those
dark specters until the sun came up,
until the needles of daylight left you.
Alone, again, with the loom.

For the first few,
all you imagined
was war.
For the last,
all you
imagined were
women

contributors

Anushka Joshi was born in Ahmedabad, India and studies history and creative writing at Sarah Lawrence College. Her first book of poems, *If Time Thinks*, was published in 2015.

Arielle Hebert holds an M.F.A in poetry from North Carolina State University. She won the 2019 North Carolina State University Poetry Contest judged by Ada Limón. Arielle believes in ghosts and magic.

Aurora Dimitre is a young author from rural North Dakota. She likes heavy metal, horror movies, and Keanu Reeves.

Greta Starling is a teenager from the United States who writes poetry and YA fiction. Her favorite poets are William Shakespeare and Natasha Trethewey.

Jocelyn Royalty is a high school senior at New Haven Academy and the Educational Center for the Arts, where she specializes in creative writing. She has been interested in the written arts since elementary school, and is dedicated to the workshop environment. She plans to study writing at the University of Maine at Farmington this coming fall.

Katie Licavoli is a Fiction and Creative Non-Fiction writer originally from Mansfield, Texas. "What Washes Up in Floods" is a chapter from a nonfiction novel-in-progress that she's been dreaming of writing for years. The novel includes a collection of unique stories from a dead-end road in the Texas countryside. She recently published her first fiction novella with BTGN.

Kristina Fedeczko received her MFA at Lesley University. Her work has appeared in *Aji Magazine, Straight Forward Poetry, Boston Accent Lit, Foliate Oak Literary Magazine* and elsewhere. When she's not writing (which is rare) she's reading, hiking, and spending time with her family and friends.

Margery Bayne is a librarian by day and a writer by night from Maryland, USA. She enjoys the literary and speculative, and she is a published short story author and an aspiring novelist. In 2012, she graduated from Susquehanna University with a BA in Creative Writing and is currently pursuing a Masters of Library Science. In her time not spent reading or writing, she enjoys origami, running, and being an aunt.

McKenzie Teter is an MFA candidate at the University of North Carolina Wilmington with a focus in poetry. Her other publications include two poems in *Her Heart Poetry's Annual Collection* (2017), a fiction piece in the *Italian Americana Review* (2019), three poems in *Voice of Eve Magazine* (2019), and one poem in *Foothill Journal* (2019).

Samantha Tetrault is a Capulet Mag editor, and she's weaseled her way into this magazine yet again. This time, in the form of a *Twilight* essay. Yikes.

Sofia Rybkina is a professional musician, artist, poet, member of the French poets society, and author of the book *Speaking in Verse* published in Russia in 2016. Her works have appeared in such journals as *Slovo\Word, La Page Blanche, Berlin. Berega,* and *Star 82 Review*. She lives and studies in Saint Petersburg.

Sophie Hamidovic is a self-taught artist and illustrator based in Nova Scotia, Canada. She uses both digital and traditional mediums, her favourites being gouache, acrylic and graphite. Sophie's work is heavily inspired by nature, along with her own personal experiences as seen through her surreal style.

editors

Isabelle Rodriguez is the poetry editor and social coordinator for Capulet Mag. She works full time at a mind numbing desk job, and spends her off time writing, podcasting, and cruising Yelp for new places to eat.

Samantha Tetrault is the nonfiction and fiction editor, as well as the print designer for Capulet Mag. She is a full-time marketing writer, blogger, and podcaster. She loves working for herself, reading bad books, and spending too much time on Reddit.

Capulet Mag is an inclusive literary magazine seeking the best in fiction, nonfiction, poetry, and art by young women.

Submit your work at CapuletMag.com